United Artists Books
114 W. 16th Street, 5C
New York, NY 10011

unitedartistsbooks.com
spdbooks.org

Morning Ritual

Lisa Rogal

United Artists Books
New York, 2015

for Vicki Rogal

Contents

IV

V

VI

"Nobody sees a flower – really – it is so small it takes time – and we haven't time – and to see takes time – like to have a friend takes time."

— Georgia O'Keeffe

I woke up this morning and ran the faucet. It was the fourth day without hot water and I suddenly wanted to kill my landlord. I took a wrench from my toolbox that I keep on an open shelf just outside the bathroom. Then I realized I didn't know what to do with the wrench to fix the problem, or if it was even something I could fix. I set the wrench on the counter where it will stay for at least a week, before I finally return it to its spot.

I woke up this morning and ran the faucet. It was the fourth day without hot water and I suddenly wanted to kill my landlord. I decided to go for a run anyway and grit through another icey shower. It was cold, so I wore leggings, a pullover, gloves, and a hat. The dog doesn't need anything but a collar and leash. We ran uphill for the first half, two clouds of hot breath escaping downwind. On the downhill I was able to get that feeling where your whole consciousness is in your head and your body runs without orders.

I woke up this morning and ran the faucet. It was the fourth day without hot water and I suddenly wanted to kill my landlord. I took a wrench from my toolbox that I keep on an open shelf just outside the bathroom, left my apartment open, went downstairs to the first floor and banged on the landlord's door. She answered on the third knock and I hit her in the face with the wrench until we were both covered in blood.

I woke up this morning and ran the faucet. It was the fourth day without hot water and I suddenly wanted to kill my landlord. I took a wrench from my toolbox that I keep on an open shelf just outside the bathroom. Then I realized I didn't know what to do with the wrench to fix the problem, or if it was even something I could fix. I tossed the wrench on the couch, where it will eventually get sucked into the cushions and I'll assume it's lost, when really, it will be right under me.

I woke up this morning and ran the faucet. It was the fourth day without hot water and I suddenly wanted to kill my landlord. I took a wrench from my toolbox that I keep under the sink in the kitchen. Then I realized I didn't know what to do with the wrench to fix the problem, or if it was even something I could fix. I set the wrench on the counter where it will stay for who knows how long. I made coffee and a bowl of cereal and took them to the couch. When I finished I sat there with the dog under my feet and stared into space until I forgot everything.

I woke up this morning and ran the faucet. It was the fourth day without hot water and I suddenly wanted to kill my landlord. I took a wrench from my toolbox that I keep on an open shelf just outside the bathroom. I bent down and began tightening the various components of the sink but they just kept getting looser and looser and soon the pipes drooped like hot wax and became long sticky strings that I tried to hold up in my hands, but when I touched them, they melted away completely.

I woke up this morning and ran the faucet. It was the fourth day without hot water and I suddenly wanted to kill my landlord. I took a wrench from my toolbox that I keep on an open shelf just outside the bathroom, left my apartment open, went downstairs to the first floor and banged on the landlord's door. She answered on the third knock. Did the man come to look at the hot water tank yet? I asked. He never showed up, she said. She looked like she hadn't showered in a month. Well? I said with my eyes and a wave of the wrench. S'pose to come today, she said. Then she shrugged and I swear I almost hit her in the face with that wrench.

I woke up this morning and didn't even check the water. I went straight out for a run, hoping when I got home it would be hot. If it wasn't, I'd have to suffer through another ice cold shower. It was an unusually warm day and I was covered in sweat when I got back. Hesitantly, I ran the water in the bathroom sink and stuck my fingers under.

I woke up this morning and ran the faucet. It was the fourth day without hot water and I suddenly wanted to kill my landlord. I took a wrench from my toolbox that I keep under the sink in the kitchen. Then I realized I didn't know what to do with the wrench to fix the problem, or if it was even something I could fix. I balanced myself with one foot inside the tub and one on the floor and swung the wrench against the tile under the shower head. The smack echoed in my skull but I kept swinging and swinging until the tile cracked and dust clouds filled the bathroom and my lungs. I began pulling chunks of tile from the wall and dropping them into the tub. A thick coat of plaster dust covered the porcelain and my skin and hair. I could feel myself swallowing it and could barely open my eyes, but I kept going until I'd made a big enough opening to get to the pipes. Unfortunately, all my wild swinging had caused damage and the pipes hissed and sputtered as freezing water poured down the wall.

I woke up this morning and ran the faucet. It was the fourth day without hot water and I suddenly wanted to kill my landlord. But instead I left her a nice note in the entryway downstairs:

> Still no hot water
> Please let me know when it might be fixed

When I came home that evening, the note was there in the entryway and I washed my dishes in ice cold water.

I woke up this morning and ran. When I got back I turned on the shower and got undressed. The run was cold and I was looking forward to a nice hot shower. After a few minutes the water was still cold. A few minutes later, it was freezing cold. I turned it off and waited fifteen minutes, but it was no better. I tried the sink in the bathroom and kitchen – both cold. I was covered in sweat, so

I stepped in the shower and turned the handle hesitantly. I jumped around under the water, hoping to get warmer and quickly washed my body and hair. Eventually, my skin got red and numb and it wasn't so bad anymore.

I woke up this morning and ran the faucet. It was the fourth day without hot water and I suddenly wanted to kill my landlord. But instead I left her a nice note in the entryway downstairs:

> Still no hot water
> Please let me know when it might be fixed

When I came home that evening, the note was there in the entryway and I washed my dishes in ice cold water. The next day, the note was still there, and the next day and the next after that. After a while I got used to the freezing cold showers and even thought of them as a necessary part of my morning routine. I realized, eventually, that I hadn't seen or heard from my landlord in several months. My rent checks piled in the entryway, uncollected. Out of guilt, I kept writing them. But there were so many – it seemed they were multiplying on their own. I finally had to collect them in a garbage bag and throw them out.

I woke up this morning and ran the faucet. It was the fourth day without hot water and I suddenly wanted to sunbathe on the roof. My landlord told me not to go up there so I slid the hatch open silently. Upstairs I discovered a forest of clothing and rats nests. I pawed my way through them to reach a clearing. I could see the whole city and the boroughs beyond and the cities and towns beyond those. I had super-sonic seeing. I saw my old playground on the top of a mountain and my old schoolyard and the factories near my old house. I saw my twelfth grade Spanish teacher clapping his hands on his pants, leaving white chalk marks. I saw the basketball court where I sprained my ankle and then I confused one uncle for another but I figured it out. I saw the My Little Ponies under my friends' beds. I saw the ferry boat I rode to a dock with my parents, it was Maine I guess. I saw my sister's bed when it became a spaceship. I saw all my old dogs when they were young and the goldfish graves we dug. I saw my first everything again. I saw the pages of my journals fluttering about. I saw the wicked witch. I saw The Navigator in Spanish and the movie theater where I went to see it. I saw the pancakes at IHOP and the diners and greasy meals and silverware and tabletops and the puffy stools and chairs. I saw all the books in stacks and stacks and the best ones in there somewhere. I saw the bed where I first had sex and the beds of my friends from way back. I saw the wax candles melting on my parents' kitchen table. I was floating in the space of all the things I'd touched and all my baby toys were visible again. I grazed a blankey with my finger tips and it was soft as a cheek, so soft my fingers felt like limestone crumbling. My skin was crumbling with everything I touched. Where was the roof? Where were my friends? I saw my friends from middle school riding go carts and some of them looked just like they did. These were not my friends. That Spanish boy I knew whispering to me Pablo baby, please come down. A group of us were playing hide and seek through the neighborhood. We'd sneaked some whiskey in our Cokes. He couldn't find me. He was misquoting his favorite band. Calling me baby in code. I saw myself wanting to hide well, but also wanting him to find me – somewhere secret. He couldn't find me. He was too stupid. I was angry at myself for hiding so well – too well for him to uncover me. I would reveal myself from now on. But I didn't. I saw all the times I failed to reveal myself. I saw the laundry hamper I used to hide behind. It only comes to my knees now. I saw the dresser I used to sleep walk to and lay behind. It was always flush to the wall again when I woke up.

I woke up this morning and ran the faucet. It was the whatever day without hot water and I couldn't remember how long it'd been since I'd had a hot shower. The dog was whining to go out and I knew my landlord would start banging on my floor if I let it go on too long. I leash up the dog and think about the forced nature of our relationship. She seems happy enough, a happy prisoner, so we walk and walk for miles from one neighborhood to the next. We walk first to Fourth Avenue and south from there under the overpasses and past the F stop and past the large red church with spires and past its fenced lawn. Churches are supposed to be welcoming but they make me feel bad like when I see a police officer. Jesus don't want me for a sunbeam, I sing in my head. The dog is trotting and happy still despite the fact that I tug on her leash when she walks ahead of me. We pass things like the U-Haul and Dunkin Donuts, McDonalds, Best Western. What are these things doing here? And what is the dog thinking down there in that head? There's a cemetery just down the street but it's really west and uphill. Eventually we turn towards the river and it smells. It's been a long walk, which I haven't designed to circle back, so we're only half-way at best. The dog wants to drink the dirty Gowanus. She pulls that way as though she's sensing water. Probably smelling the dead edges of the island. After this walk a hot shower would be the best and I list all the things that have to happen before that happens.

I woke up this morning and ran the faucet. It was the fourth day without hot water and I suddenly wanted to kill my landlord. But instead I just think bitch bitch bitch bitch while I hop around under the freezing water for a minute or two. In the mirror, I find shampoo suds in my ear and wipe them away. The coffee is hot, so this is good. I hug it to my chest and promise to be grateful. Then I stub my toe on the coffee table and yell. The dog tilts her head up at me from the couch. I remember my dream all of a sudden. It's with me while I walk to the train and take the train two stops to work because it's cold out and walk from the train to the building and show my ID and go inside and take the stairs in twos because the elevator's slow and the stairs are better exercise and sit at a computer and open my email. I stare at the screen for several minutes trying to remember the rest of the dream. A man's face with a faint mustache. Something that happened on a plain – brown and dotted with those short Californian trees like the ones on the highway between Sacramento and San Francisco. I sit there and feel the feeling it's left as strongly as possible because I know it'll be gone soon. Driving down an empty highway cutting through a flat wide open plain, brown and dotted with those short Californian trees like the kind on the highway between Sacramento and San Francisco, though none of the hills. Headed somewhere I'm not supposed to be going, but I'm excited to be going. Thrilled by an unknown danger. At times I'm driving and at times it's this vague face with the slight mustache. A hat. A large hand on the wheel. We're talking about something – this is the key to the dream – about where we're headed and the reason and I also brought up the scenery and how great it was and something may have happened in the sky. Someone else enters the shared office and we make small talk for a few minutes and then the dream is gone, though the details I've uncovered remain, but really they mean nothing now and even seem a bit ridiculous.

I woke up this morning and ran the faucet. I let the faucet run and run and the sound and sight of continual water turns into a trance. I keep inserting my fingers into the stream to see it ruined and restored over and over. I want to ruin it over and over forever and play with it to make it become other things. It insists on being water, on being movement and stillness at once, on coming forever though eventually it will end, if it runs long enough it will run out, eventually though it seems to go on forever, in a way it seems not to be moving though I can sort of see it moving, sort of not. It's moving and not, it's new water every second though it looks just the same as always, until I put my fingers in and disrupt its stream, but my disruption is never enough. It goes right back to its place. I can only throw it off track for a second. That second feels so good, I want to make it permanent. I want to break the stream. I want to crush the water in a fist – that doesn't work. I want to push the water aside, to push it into a new shape. I want to assure myself that it's actually flowing, changing, not one of those frozen fountains meant to look like moving water. I want it to stop being what it is for a second, so I can really see it.

I woke up this morning and ran the faucet. It was the fourth day without hot water. Some people never have hot water, I thought, and was proud of myself for being so aware and grateful, though secretly I wanted to kill my landlord.

I woke up this morning and ran the faucet. It was the final day without hot water, I promised myself. Tomorrow I'd have a hot shower and my skin would be soothed of this terrible cold. I would stand in the water for hours if that's what it took. I would threaten not to pay rent until the hot water returned, which is what my friends said I should do though I could never bring myself to do it. I kept paying rent as the cold water days continued until it was summer and a cold shower was just what I wanted. The summer made me let go of my promise. I got spring fever my friends said because all I wanted were cold showers and hot men. I became a new person in the spring and summer, a person who loves cold showers, a person whose skin always feels smooth and damp. I began to make love in the shower, to eat in the shower, take naps there, read and write as well, all with the cold, fresh water running down on me, though the books, the food, the blankets and pillows I'd collected in the tub never seemed to get wet. How could someone do a thing like this, I asked. I asked that a lot as the news, the gossip, the emails, the stories reached me in my shower-house. When the fall became winter I moved out.

I woke up this morning and ran the faucet. It was the fourth day without hot water and I suddenly wanted to kill my landlord, in the figurative sense of course. Some people never have hot water, I said to myself and tried to hang on to that thought. I thought of Spain in the coldest months when I had no hot water or heat, only a space heater I could turn on for ten minutes after dinner, any more and my señora would yell fuego, fuego. But we laid our bras across it in the morning anyway, warming up the cups. It wouldn't be so bad if you had a chance to warm up at some point in the day, but few buildings had heat and they were lined with tiles to keep things cool in the summer. Walking across Saint Elmo bridge in a ski parka as the sun rose – on my way out or on my way home – is the thing I remember most.

I woke up this morning and ran the faucet. It was the
fourth day without hot water and I mentally cursed my
landlord. But I had things to do – I had to walk the dog,
she was staring at me. On our walk we ran into Pauline,
who I knew from the Blarney Cove. Everyone had called
her a witch because of her huge black hair and long black
dresses with full sleeves and her crazy eyes rimmed with
thick liner. There was a picture of her behind the bar, her
wrinkles illuminated by the flash, her eyes like an animal
caught in the night. She once drowned a mouse under the
faucet in the sink. It's struggling, she yelled to the regu-
lars. As I passed her I raised my hand and smiled, then I
slowed down and said her name. She didn't even look, just
rolled her wheelie suitcase down the cracked sidewalk,
eyes blazing.

I woke up this morning and ran the faucet. It was the
fourth day without hot water and I suddenly wanted to
cry. I decided I needed something to cheer myself up
– a reminder of summer. My first thought was to take
the train out to Long Island and see the ocean, how it
looked in the snow. I didn't have time, I knew that, but I
let myself fantasize about it for a while. The dog looked
miserable in the corner. I had to walk her even though the
thought of walking in the snow and wind made me feel
helpless. This is a simple thing, I said to myself. This is an
easy life. But it would be so much easier if I had hot water,

or a yard, or lived in Hawaii. I thought of Mexico – the men walking down the beach with split mangoes on sticks. I decided to stop in the bodega and buy a mango on my walk. They always have them even out of season, if you're willing to pay three dollars. Jack says never pay more than a dollar for a mango, which is easy to say when you live in California. He says he taught me how to eat mango. He showed me how to cut it – to find the pit and insert the knife as close as possible along the sides. To dice it inside the peel and pop it out like this. But he means he taught me how to like it. He says he doesn't know what I ate before I met him. In Mexico, we camped on the beach in the small, dirty crescent of sand with local tourists and old men fishing from the shore at four in the morning, frying fish for the Mexican families camping beside us. In the afternoon they came out with the mangoes on sticks, peeled and diced so their pulp skirted out from the center in circular rows. It was only the first day we were willing to pay for mangoes. The other days we climbed the rocks on the south side of the beach and found coconuts that had fallen from the trees on the hill above. It takes longer than you'd think to crack them open. First you have to find a sharp rock, then you have to saw a divot into the shell, then smash it and smash it against the rock until there is a crack wide enough for your fingers. Then you pry until your fingers are sore, then smash again until the outer shell cracks open. After that you have to knock it gently with a small rock so you don't bust open the inner shell and lose all the milk inside. The coconut did not compare to the mangoes, but we ate it while I told him a story he didn't know yet about kindergarten when a man came to give us coconut and I had to leave early so I didn't get to drink the coconut milk – though Mrs. King gave me a little baggy of coconut meat that was hot by the time I ate it and very disappointing. Jack wrestled a white chunk away from the husk. But the one day we did get the mango it was so good that later I wished I'd never tasted it, because after that whenever I saw the men eating with their faces jutting out so the juice didn't drip on their bare chests, I knew how good it was, ripe in just the right way. The good ones like that are hard to find in the city, the period between ripeness and rot only a sliver of time. In the bodega they had them stiff and green or gummy or mushy, hinting at decay. I picked the best one I could find – it has to have a little bit of red, Jack says. It tasted funny, but I ate it anyway.

Wow this is pretty
Under the arch of trees
You can't even think about anything
Under this arch of trees

A moon of substance
A moon of substance
What can be bothering me

The guy at the fish counter was a huge jerk today
Why do they always have to act like they know everything

Well, darling
It's often hard
Under this arch of trees
The springtime has your number

The snapper's not its color
Under this arch of trees
Well, darling
What can be bothering me
It's not so hard
Being pretty
You can't even think
Under the pretty trees

How many hopeful monsters
Over the bridge
Dead little city

Behind the silver
Moon of substance
People don't notice
A subway confection
Up here the air is ready to breathe

It's nice to have leggings on and then to put something over the leggings so as not to be cold / to pull the leg warmers up or put the long sweater around the hips and thighs so as not to be cold / to be warmer in the spots covered by something in addition to leggings / and slightly cold in the other spots / say the middle thighs / to think of the legs in leggings / partially covered by things above and below / in a sexual way / to see them as sexual parts / being covered but less than other parts / this is sexual in its way / to have a part exposed between other parts / to see these parts as sexual for a moment / then not / then a way to be warm or cold / or partially warmed in an extra / comforting way / then again to see them as sexual parts / particularly the part of the thigh not warmed / the middle thigh which only has leggings covering it / to see this part as its own part / sexualized in relation to the parts of the leg with both leggings and another layer for warmth / it is nice to do this and to go back and forth in your thinking of the part / its various ways of being

It's nice to linger in obsession / until it becomes not nice / to go back and forth in your perception of the thighs / particularly the middle thighs which are covered by leggings but nothing else / and then in relation to the parts with extra covering / on the one hand / as a sexualized part in this configuration / on the other hand / simply a means to experience warmth or cold in slight degrees of each other / in close proximity on the body / it is nice when no one's watching / to see the two ways back and forth / the border between the two ways nearly gone / both / both ways of being / then to

see someone in the woods / on a bike between the trees
and wonder if it is really a bike / which between trees / on
that uneven part of the woods / behind the house would
be difficult / and then to wonder what you were thinking
of / just before this man on his bicycle arrived

A guide to dying and what else
A horn in the cigarette
Mere change
Only what's real
Can become a dream

I may unconsciously reveal myself
Some party
What is the mechanism reaching out

A table between us
Some people
Temporary properties of fields
A stream of numbers
A number of streams
Something's happening
To give the world substance

I was dreaming of a party of women / all on the floor / what were we doing there / were babies and bodily functions / a chaperone in a square hat / in the corner / in a dark chair / a laughing man / mostly still / there was a sense that you couldn't leave / except for a minute to use the bathroom / there was a sense that you were children who were women / there was a sense of being half-dressed for a reason / I wanted to look at the other women but there was no communication / just smiling / playing / or sleeping or pretending

I woke up this morning in the middle of an odd and fascinating dream – so abruptly that I was angry and tried to fall back asleep to regain the moment. I had been working as some sort of spy or agent. My job was to go to bars to track down information from certain important people and for some reason to do this I required a chaperone who was an old man at the end of the bar who refused to acknowledge me. We weren't supposed to reveal that we knew each other. I guessed as much because I hadn't been told this in advance. My task was to convince certain people I was interested in going home with them, and somehow, through this deception, uncover things they did not want to reveal about themselves. What, exactly, I needed to uncover, I wasn't sure. My chaperone was supposed to have told me, but he was still refusing to acknowledge me. Any time I glanced in his direction, he looked away, or he blew smoke in my face.

I was looking for the important people, but I had no idea who they were, so I struck up a conversation with the bartender who materialized into the barista from the coffee shop where I go to write. I was relieved to see someone I knew. I had been unsure how to order my drink – everyone at this bar spoke Swedish – a rum and coke which I hate in real life, though I was really craving it in the dream. I knew this barista spoke English so I ordered in English. He presented me with a coffee mug full of some chocolate drink which he then sprayed with a hairdryer that caused white fog to materialize inside the rim of the mug. For a minute I thought he didn't speak English after all but then I realized he was giving me a special treat as an acknowledgement that we knew each other from someplace else.

I could feel my chaperone glaring at me from down the bar. At first I thought he was chastising me for ignoring my assignment, but then I realized this was a signal. Three people at the table behind me began calling my name. I ignored them. I was not supposed to be me. I was worried the barista might get suspicious. I wanted to ask the chaperone what to do, but he had resumed his distant behavior. I interpreted his glare to mean the barista was a target. Though I was sure I was looking for people with money – I couldn't remember why, but my gut told me that the end result of this mission was to somehow get money from people. The barista in his white T-shirt and shorts was glaringly out of place. I suddenly felt the need to hide him.

I told him I was unable to pay for my drink – my chaperone was also supposed to have given me money – and this worked as a signal to him. He showed me to a door by the bar and told me to go all the way to the bottom of the stairs behind this door and wait for him. When I opened the door there were no stairs leading down, only up. So I waited for him inside the landing. He opened the door and gave me a severe, disappointed look. The three people yelling at me from the table saw me standing inside the doorway, which I took to be a failure of some kind – possibly a dangerous one.

We went up the stairs together. He was holding a suit jacket that did not match his outfit. By about the fifth landing, I realized that the jacket belonged to my chaperone. There were two possibilities: he had killed the chaperone, or they were on the same side – the barista was one of us. I asked him but instead of answering me, he pushed my back so that I flew up the last set of stairs into a wooden loft. There was a tiny door leading into an apartment, but we stayed huddled in the wooden loft, waiting.

This is when my alarm clock went off and I tried to force myself back to sleep. I needed to know what had happened to my chaperone, if the barista was a good or bad guy, if I was a good or bad guy, what we were waiting for up there, if we would ever go into the apartment. But I couldn't get back into the dream. I did fall asleep for a little longer, but I dreamed I was waking up, picking out a shirt, getting dressed. I was irritated when the snooze went off that not only had I been unable to re-enter the dream but I was not dressed already and was late.

I walk my dog for 45 minutes. I pretend, for her sake, that I know what direction I'm going, but I usually decide based on the crosswalk lights. If the little white man tells me to go left on Fourth Avenue, I do. If the orange hand forces me to keep walking towards Third, then I do that. I can't let it go on like this forever, or I might never get home, but I let it go on long enough to make the walk at least 30 minutes – this seems like a reasonable amount of time for a walk. On the other hand, in the scheme of an entire day 30 minutes is a very short time to do the one thing that makes you happy, which for her is walking. Eating sure, but that takes five minutes tops, usually less. So I try to add another 30 minute walk at the end of the day, if I'm not too tired.

Today we see a little French boy find a coke bottle on the sidewalk. He tries to pick it up and hand it to his mother, but she scolds him. He laughs – from shock it seems – and drops it. She makes him pick it up and put it back where he found it, which is weird because it's obviously garbage. She could have made him put it in the recycling bins on the sidewalk. He runs to her and she grabs his wrist, as if his hand is filthy from touching the bottle. My dog sniffs his stomach where his shirt has come up and I pull her away because parents usually don't like that, but the mother smiles and says wow, wow as we pass.

Later there is an older man pushing a stroller with a woman who is much younger than him. He asks her why all the cars are parked like that and she explains to him about alternate side parking – though she does it in a very confusing way and I don't think he understands. He must be the woman's father, visiting from somewhere to see her and his grandkid, asleep in the stroller he's pushing. It reminds me I haven't spoken to my parents in a while and I should probably call them.

When I get home I eat a bowl of cereal and drink coffee

– I read while I'm doing it which is why many of my books have coffee stains in the pages. But this morning I don't spill – at least not noticeably. I want another cup of coffee, but I have to get ready or I'll be late. In the shower, I can't stop thinking about my dream. I had forgotten it on the walk, but pieces are returning to me now that had slipped away: my chaperone blew perfect smoke rings out his nostrils; the barista stuck his hand up my shirt while we were ascending the stairs – I felt I should act offended but I let him continue – then he pulled out one of those plastic things that attach price tags to clothing, which was both a relief and a disappointment; there was an old lady at the bar in a burgundy dress with short, bleached hair who I knew, when our eyes met, was doing the same thing as me.

The subway is packed with commuters this time of day. I squeeze into a seat and the woman to my right pulls her arm away when my jacket brushes it.

I have work to do; I do it. I teach a class. Before home I stop in the coffee shop to write. The barista is there. It is odd to see him in real life now, having had this dream the night before. He looks different, but exactly the same – the way a celebrity looks when you see them on the street. I keep stealing glances at him and it's coming off all wrong. I force myself to stop. I am really bad about staring. Aside from making people uncomfortable, it can get you into trouble. A man will approach, thinking I'm flirting. Many women do not appreciate another woman staring at them.

They take it as an insult. Now I'm worried the dream will cost me my favorite coffee shop. The barista keeps looking over here. He is wondering what my glances mean. He comes by and asks if I need anything. No, fine, I say, but then I wish I had asked for something because it would explain the staring. I have a manic moment where I imagine blurting out my entire dream to him – even the part about the bra tag. I laugh out loud a little because I can't help it. It's bizarre. The thought embarrasses me, but it's also an exciting possibility. There aren't enough people here to distract from my odd behavior. I force myself to be normal for the next half hour, then I leave slyly.

I read for a while before bed. My apartment is cold. They haven't turned the heat on yet and they probably won't for a few more weeks at least. I invite the dog up next to me on the couch and she squeezes in, making her body skinny and long. She is warm against my side; her fur smells like a blanket my grandmother would lay over me when I was little and I fell asleep at her house.

I read a poem that's about
a piano from a movie a silent
film by a woman
that's about domestic-
ation vacations shown in maga-
zines like the librarian makes
coffee for me and removes
her glasses her long wool
skirt brushes my knee I'm
in a movie about
satisfaction or longing or knowing
we're outside
reality in the grip of a future
situation that never
happens she undresses and
becomes someone else entirely
now like a porno
woman that hardness
was there all along beneath the soft
material of air I am
attracted through her sweater
I see her heart beating it's just
on the surface of a placid
skin if you want to see
a great movie don't see
yourself sitting
in the dark with all these
people riding a nightmare
to the end after

you've woken so that it will
not never end will
disappear like a puff
of cigar air a cherry tip in
your fortune a Mary's kitchen
phone tip she twirled the curled cord
around her finger before he entered
a little flirtation is nothing like I am
not this person you see here or I am
often seeing things through your lens

at the salvage shop
they had oodles of windows and doors
I stole a door   sketched
the name in wood with a Swiss Army Knife   a gift
to please any active
          man   it said LISA
when I was through   I've got a story
how I stole each of you
dressed you the same   and released you
at the open-air mall
          which makes us all
feel rich or poor   the luxury
of the movie theater's
purple sprawl

Words are use-objects
You are decorative
I want delineation
Here we don't spell check
Female dogs are bitches 'n hos
Women and dogs are words
The night stand's toe is broken
Those fake claw foots
It's a Taser   so look out
This window is covered in soot
Soot   a thing of the past
I have to maintain my boundaries
We   a way to disappear
Periods come from somewhere mysterious
We're afraid our rooms will explode
I can wake up in whatever I dream I'm wearing
Please pause for signals
Children are not little stanzas
We're all a bunch of fuck-heads ourselves
I don't want to talk about myself
You want to touch the mystery
Please do not please me 'till I hate you
Women are useful and dogs are a bunch of boneheads
The moth ashes under fingers
Color me a coral sea
A cockroach came out the sinkhole
My mind opens up and sucks down the scene
I have to be quiet for a while excuse me
Oxygen journeys to overused   underused brain cells both

The baby's growing cells on a daily basis
There's some anger out there in general

in the bookstore the boys saw me pawing through pages /
they were with me / with their eyes / through the shop I
stopped reading / kept faking / watching the page / turn-
ing occasionally / trying to act cool

certain things stick to you / you can't see without a little
light / a little orange mood light / like you find on the
nightstand of someone you didn't know / had so much /
sensory intelligence

a scent that hits you walking in the city can conjure any il-
lusion / crush it in the park / leave it in the park even if no
one ever finds it / because it's there / that either matters or
not / on the balance with everything else

We're drunk from drinking the universe
Blackness like a Sunday afternoon
In any season humming
As we move beneath the surface
Of skin porous I want
To know what everyone wants
To know what you imagine   pull back
Before thought was so powerful some people
Think that's what happens   whatever they say
Will happen   did these things happen
Before you   if you   take it
Slowly it's more   effective
The medicine adapts to the
Arm   arm accepts what's hurt
Before   this time things feel
All different/divine

here's poetry
this morning clumsily
she made herself
endearing my dear
dear earring my dear
ring

well but
we're all friends
here and
you can't
fall off
Mister Floor

but it can always get
worse the theory what
if the worst thing
that happens hasn't happened
yet what if
the worst thing happens
it's you
bite your lip
in the same spot
you bit before

I just want to hold
the book to my chest
such a sorry sack you were
right about that

oh balls
where'd you go
I know
I'm a woman but still
we can all
have balls if we
try they say
it's up to you

I'm talking nihilism
I'm talking botany
I'm talking television
I'm talking Nazis
I'm talking talking
I'm talking Vaseline
I'm talking glasses
          two pairs for less
I'm talking pamphlets
I'm talking hats that say wigwam
I'm talking my hat that says wigwam
          here I am
I'm talking about my hat sitting on the table
          it's harder to make something
          it's always harder to make something
          is what I'm talking about
I'm talking service industry
I'm talking jargon
I'm talking noodles
I'm talking about what you're talking about
          we're all talking noodles
I'm talking come on home
I'm talking a nugget of self
I'm talking about my Jambox
I'm talking socialism
          euphemism
          my government – mine
I'm talking give it here

I'm talking about myself now in third person
                as in her over there
I'm talking a sliver of hot pink nail
                  polish dripped on her bare
                  thigh
I'm talking lineage
I'm talking soft wet magic
I'm talking about the perfect bite
I'm talking poetry as sex
                where do you turn
I'm talking pimps now for a while
I'm talking cookies n' cream gelato
I'm talking you
                have a different experience
                than me   different reality
I'm talking yeah
                isn't it true   and well
                I have to reject interesting things though
                they're nice to think about
I'm talking look how far we've come guys
I'm talking bottomless hunger
I'm talking bottomless coffee
                on Tuesdays
I'm talking sculpture – scripture – sculpture
I'm talking a degree in architecture
I'm talking surprise
I'm talking systems as in
                my system is overloaded

        my sprinkler system is broke

        my system for study involves Adderall

I'm talking tokens

I'm talking half off on all merchandise

I'm talking haven't you read it

I'm talking New Year's blank

I'm talking calcium supplements

        I always forget them in the morning

        morning's rough

I'm talking do me a favor

I'm talking about my hair in this weather

I'm talking laundry

I'm talking philosophies of love

I'm talking this season's prospects

I'm talking about a gift I once got

I'm talking about not wanting anything

I'm talking each line a rhyme

        I don't know why

I'm talking about the secret – shh!

I'm talking about we're sharing secrets and it feels so good

I'm talking about me now for a while again

        what did you say

I'm talking about a mile a minute

I'm talking about an apple a day

I'm talking about not talking anymore

        but I keep talking about it

I'm talking someone being intimidated

        by someone

                    you know very well
                    and feel comfortable with
     I'm talking solitude
                    loneliness
                    adrenaline junkies
                    white outs
                    damages
                    to property and cost of living
     I'm talking   fine
     I'm talking empathy
                    and how we will unwind
     I'm talking about the candles burned to
                    the wick in the night
     I'm talking space heater – space heater
                    fire because
                    we laid
                    our cold bras across it
     I'm talking cupping warm mugs
                    your hands are freezing
     I'm talking all these phrases
                    living with me
     I'm talking a thing

                              you can't escape

     I'm talking Tahiti

                    close your eyes
                    to what you can't imagine

anyway
what are you doing
what's up

okay, great

let's all talk in a circle
and forget
your face makes me think
of a man's against mine
my Maya Deren
dear my love the
way children and
babies are mine
or hers if she finds them
in the phone unhung
there is no gravity to this
music a woman can fall
wanting the nun – look your way
there is no one but you
in the mirror where
slivers of sunlight
blind little brute
his woman
told me a song
sung by the old
women veiled and foggy – old women
only care about comedy
all the women – electrically veiled
performing rituals
at the night stand
little white cloud dress
little white nothing
in the back room
the God's in the breast

equal when two
heroes salute they
mirror each other
with their sacred
rattles to show
respect – the colors
naked something between
the meal – hand held
to the throat – thigh
stockings pulled to the
edge all the wet
descent
legs down a new
soft morning
after some Spanish
casa white knives
puddle of the star
salutes really in a
fortress now tell me
the truth – tell me the
painful truth – the skirts
ah
thing that can
contain you
rise you up – relief
as in
a wealth of
frozen foods

I'm obsessed with teenagrrlz
because they seem so   very
in a way   daddy made you
she said to herself
in the park   park
of ears   park of bugs
remember last year
when I was having
a bad day

I'm reading a book
a poet with hair
thinking of a painter on her period
a fire that consumes all before it
well I don't have to like it
half plain   half everything
nothing could come close to capturing
the little chocolates
got in bed with me
I've ruined the evening/everything

their husbands stare
not because I'm young/pretty
I'm a different
faux   mystery
the waitress could see
I was in agony   but I was
sick   in the hood
now said the tour guide   playing Fresh Prince
and no one waved
it was cold   these kids
never seen so many
people/fraternity

where she took her socks off
to walk uphill
drunk on a rock
the cold can get you
though you don't

see it   she is dead
sexy   behind the peephole
her stomach   an entrance
the section on slavery/mid-section a slab

only the guards are black   she asks him
to explain the paintings
she eyes him   she's only kidding
he knew a lot of paintings
I heard her   outside the academy
he tried to touch her
arm   lost the nerve
you can walk into the painting
this is the future
you can look into that hole
I can't say what's inside/we're all different

I'm talking   a beer   and so
                        more things
I'm talking park beneath a tree
                        the daily is like walking
I'm talking the air   the jam
                        as in   that's it
I'm talking moon moon   oh man
                        this most interesting
                        word clash
I'm talking more than ever
I'm talking the bells
                        and kinda going all over
I'm talking cup of coffee
                        all around me
                        mound of me

    I am not
cool like them
gathering
in a house
        I see them when
you play me
Wolf is on
the Hill on the Angel
Melodyhorn   with wine
and chords in the chorus
        as if we go
to church   hear organs
through the skin   ski in
ski out   that's what it's
all about

Sometimes you have to say to yourself
        today was a long day
Sometimes you have to go to sleep though
        everything whispers listen
Sometimes silver magic ships they carry
        all those colors to your dreams
Sometimes you are being sentimental
        which is selfish
Sometimes everything is selfish
Sometimes you can't remember what to say or how
Sometimes you forget your life
        what life looks like and what yours is
Sometimes there's thunder
        that becomes a motorcycle
Sometimes you write the lyrics of songs into the poem
        and don't give them credit
Sometimes credit is weak
Sometimes you lose your job two weeks before Christmas
Sometimes religious people knock on the door
        and ask to give you the word of Jesus
Sometimes you want to let them in
        for tea or just to see what the word is
        what it's all about
        or watch the struggle
        of the pitch
Sometimes you want to stop
        and dive
        into the water where foam is nudging
        for the sick pleasure of feeling disgusting

disgusted at foam on skin
Sometimes things don't get done like they should
Sometimes the tea is bitter
though I steeped it just three minutes
Sometimes the religious people they
complain about the tea
Sometimes you want nothing
neat and connected
Sometimes people know the truth about life
or they find out later
Sometimes I do something gross I won't
tell you about
Sometimes the imagination is worse and acts as a mirror
Sometimes you have to let yourself off the hook
you put yourself on it
Sometimes punctuation is a crutch for the mind
Sometimes I spot one tiny ant body moving along
the lip of the tub
in the sunlight it seems like
a sign of friendship on a
strange morning
then I see two three four
more in various corners and their
numbers destroy the intimacy
Sometimes I scrunch my shoulders up consistently
Sometimes you leave things out to make it more seductive
Sometimes you figure something out
Sometimes I'm up early
up so early that no one

                    seems alive
Sometimes we take off from the wrong place
                    and find ourselves in the air
                    unsure of who we are
Sometimes the border's arbitrary and incomplete
Sometimes I use we to show you that I care
Sometimes you laugh where no one else can laugh
                    you laugh on instinct
Sometimes you make love in the middle of the night
                    and then
                    go to IHOP
Sometimes it's too hot to be lonely
Sometimes when friends are not
                    around you sit outside
                    and listen
                    to all the birds
                    all the different kinds

I made dinner and cleaned the dishes so efficiently because I was in love. These are feelings I didn't think I could feel, a friend said to me, after a girl broke his heart. I didn't think I could feel them either, for a long time, until I did. But looking back, I actually felt them very young. Those few years before seemed to go on forever and ever, even now, they are still going on, stretching into infinity without me.

I would see my friends in love. My one friend was in love with her boyfriend. He was so cute and so dumb. I didn't understand how she could be in love with him actually. He was so very dumb. He was the most attractive guy on the dance floor. They were the most attractive couple, dancing like they were in love, looking at each other and moving together as if they knew each other's bodies like their own. I was watching them from the corner. How could they be in love? Mostly I wondered about her. What did she talk to him about? Didn't she feel that wall inside when you try to talk to him? And how did he know her? What did he say to her when they were alone? Probably there wasn't much talking. They were always touching, never talking. Always pet names and car rides on the hot spring days after school. Beer and the river. These things make you feel in love but you know deep down it isn't true. She seemed to believe it, looking at him and lifting up her dress to dance more vigorously, her hand wrapped around his neck. He had shaggy hair that fell over her hand and the dumbest, sweetest expression.

If she could be in love like this, in this way that seemed
impossible with whoever happened to be there, then I
could too. I could fake it, as they say, until I make it. I
could go to the river with his windows popped out and
our damp skin in the heavy air and smoke weed and make
out on the shore and it would be like it was anyone, like it
was me in my own head, the physical manifestation of my
inner life. He could have a blank, dumb expression and say
offensive things that I'd ignore because I'd be in love with
his body – the way it felt and smelled and moved in the
water, his torso twisted in the water like an animal I could
love from afar, from a place in my mind that respected
the distance between our worlds, even when he'd lay on
top of me with his tan body, his messy hair, a moment of
interspecies relation, which doesn't expect much and is
in that way never disappointed, because how close can
we be without language, without the chemical deception.
He drove me home in wet clothes after the loud insects
came out, his car a place of comfort for being so simple
and practical, a true example of the usefulness in living
this life. She was always getting rides and looked so happy
in the window, like a child who spent the day running
and swimming in the wild and is now headed home for
a bath and a plate of food. She said how good he was at
sex. I believed her and wondered what he did that was so
good. There were things I could imagine. I was imagining
something specific, but I didn't know what it was either.
Mostly having to do with his chest and stomach, his hands
and mouth, how it would move. His hands up in her blond

hair – they were both so tan. I could never be that tan. This was another world where I did not belong, not being free and easy in the humid air. It was such a struggle, all day long, to move. That sweet dewy skin of the others, the ease of acceptance of everything: gnats and lawn clippings and hot bleacher seats and ham biscuits and boys with hair in their eyes and never any rain to cool it down, never any end to days that seemed to keep going into the evening and even at night when I'd put my feet off the bed to escape the heat, the static air was all around.

I didn't really understand how teenagers were all about sex. I thought about sex all the time, too, so I didn't understand the disconnect, why I was never that engaged in the real acts. There was a strange, numb fogging over that came on whenever we did things. This was reality and it felt so foreign. His body felt like a big mass, not a smooth, turning animal. My body felt stuck as though I'd twisted my neck. I didn't know, at the time, the control of the inner life and assumed that reality was outside of me, that I didn't behave right in reality and so nothing felt real as it seemed to for others. I did not want to give in to my inner life, to accept its reality. I wanted to have a go of it in the real world, but nothing happened like I imagined. There was so much distance that I forgot how to act and could not relate to those external floating bodies, his finger inside me, a shock in a dream.

It wasn't until later, when I accepted the unacknowledged

world, that I felt right. I could see myself in the mirror and panic and then relax. Panic in my feelings of love that seemed to overwhelm all sense of reality and understand the panic as a message passing from one side to the other, getting across the lines, getting the lines all crossed, approaching the membrane, forcing sensation through.

look at all these quiet women
look at this substantial moon

the face of a moon
is a sideways woman

why are we always talking
here we are on a spring night

let's not talk to each other at all
we can look at each other I think

without thinking at all
what's up?

here we are about to hear poems
why are we talking / what are we

talking / what's all the
talking / in code

we're talking / let's
read and translate / let's

code / red / we're reading
these poems we're talking

to blank-faced women
when you talk to the moon who

listens but the moon and maybe
some trees we're talking to

trees all night tall bark of men
with heads of women shaking

themselves in the dark / leaves
can be dark or bright / leaves

shake and fall / what is the purpose of
this beautiful tree

it's haunting me all night
while we're talking / I want to talk

about this tree but no one will
listen / you have to talk

about trees in silence / in silence
the night keeps moving

past all cigarettes and flirtation
past all basketball and foam past all boots past all stones

past all invented creatures wine and tacos
drums / spirits / spring / paintings

and pages and faces and ear
rings and Diet

Cokes and ice
cream / we go for a cone

we're talking spring
and families / hiding all night

in the lit city lit sidewalk
café light / bar dome

homeless / homeless us
never going home

lit us / never going out
little us / we try to crack open

on the street outside the bar
our bare selves

jitter on the sidewalk
lay down on the sidewalk

convulse
a spirit got you

The air is just warm like that / like sometimes what I'm writing turns out to be a poem / a new thought enters all the time / but it's an old thought / also it's a beautiful day outside / the house is cold somehow / around here they never think of anything / to place the windows in such a way / to retain the cool air while the day gets hot / this is a place where the air stays completely still / people can break it with their voices / but there are so few people / so few noises / the air just sitting there / as if / it doesn't exist anymore / the blackest black appears like a hole in the chest / I wash all of his black t-shirts one day / I wash everything on cold because it gets just as clean / I think / when they see a black person around here it's really an event / it makes you feel strange / it's strange to feel complicit / when you don't exist / constrained by silence / a strange place / the houses all fall apart / the exterior / and no one cares / they painted the houses last summer but left big gaps / as if to say / this is enough / you get the idea / there's a giant hole in our ceiling / but nothing comes in / so no one cares / no one sees it but us / it's just by the door / some people are so friendly / but when I try to be friend-ly it doesn't work / you have to be local / have to know where you're from / I guess I'm from somewhere / but I'm not sure / constantly living in a place I don't really live / or living in two places at once / or more / some people / seem not to be going anywhere but they still get there / two people / look just like lovers / until they get close / then I see they are strangers / going the same direction / a ghost town / there are store fronts but nothing inside / or the windows are covered so I can't tell what's in there / they're closed / it's Monday / they are closed every day / when I'm here / maybe they open as soon as I make my way home / sometimes you suddenly find a group of people / a pop-up food stand out of somebody's pick-up / they all knew to be here / but I found it by accident / no one looks at me as I order a sausage / everyone has ordered something else / there is always information missing / I often think / I recognize a person / but it's somebody else / these people seem surprised they don't know me / where did I come from / what do I do with my time / I feel unsure / freeing the beetle from the web / I had put it there / it was in my hair / I thought it was a flower at first / I dropped it on the ledge / on the web / then I realized what it was / what I'd done / now the spider won't eat / but he wouldn't have / anyway / the web looks old / as all webs

I can't help but be of two minds / three minds
like a tree / all white
no leaves to lose / no birds
some of these trunks smell like alcohol
no skin / it gets you nowhere
the shapeless landscape follows me
this whole country
was meant for you and me
then who needs birth control
the shopping mall
is the place to hide
work ethic deserted
slipping off in a crowd
and you'll never get over it
or you will / so what
we are supposed to love / because
we're incorrigible / well
this is me
home like a leash
but if I was always alive I would always be
bored with everything
there's a pit / you just can't have
after all / all
the little noises
of the future

You might say
that all my loving can be
twisted into something I
don't recognize that song
I've heard a thousand
rushing water particles
in a little place with a little shore
a little river leaving me
from the center away
the streaks of light
down tracks until it fades
a ticket takes you
a way that stands for
bills bucks I've got
two bucks won't
fuck I touched the antlers
tall and vibrant those bones
vibrate while they're still
alive and after feel them
animal up there fills
silence with a smother
all the cities on me
sharp and tall
on my heads
that's poetry
each person split in three
each question end is
nothing now I'll
be in a head

of mine type
loudly to the hidden
animals hidden like
rising dead
those funny people
want to repeat the seduction
of letting it repeat
the desire of doing
nothing not doing
the thing in the dream never
having a minor moment is
dying maybe like he said his
tie must be imperfect
against his neck the
neck erotic and so many
cultures idolize the feet have you
heard women asking men their sex
fantasies they only offer
body parts floating
through space disjointed
leg torso hollow
collar bone long and
vibrant across the chest

I'd pull mine out and show
in a dream what's under
the skin so perfectly dissect-
ed from fat and bone
I'm in this for real my

minor place in theory
but every terrible
thing a relief no really a little
pain fulfilled the body
you just have to be
funny in the dark
don't you while I'm trying
to sleep for good-
ness sake my mother's
mother said those older
women ancestors keep
sitting in a passive
permanence like deer
inside the wolf out back
I'll look straight into the
woods but what
would I see there
are always
other voices
beside this

I'm lucky for a tomato / tomatoes
I'm looking for one / them
That / the one that / got away
Under the table in a dream / dreams
I had a long / long time ago of a tiny
Tiny man living under the radiator with / which
A tomato to lean on / as support
And all one's meals/z
Those green stripes of the
Past Sacramentos and still tomatoes / still tomatoes

Then this will happen
then this will happen
It will be very convenient

To finally stop talking is a surprising
blessing / the dog must be

So annoyed with us
we never stop

What's important
when you can't talk

I click my tongue all the time
now / out on the lawn

Some young women look so young
it seems like a physical disaster

To encounter another
person's body

Suddenly you saw me
in a new way / after many years

There's so much time to think
when you only talk important things

Do the necessary
thing for the moment / guess what

Every day I realize more and more
what a shit I am

No / no / please
this is a good thing

When I saw myself
after a long time I realized

I was completely not
me again

This long distraction may become
the main thing

Blow to the face / swift maneuver / cut back / attack of
civility
please don't believe me

When I tell you
how it is

You wouldn't see any
hippie baby here

Hips moving like a Libra
supple limb movement / in the cool shade of the hottest
day

They've ever seen / my memory
going nowhere / such a goldfish

Let me tell you something
about today

It's definitely
happening

A lot of things happened today. I mean, I feel I exhausted
the day in some sense, seeing as I started it one way and
transformed several times since then. I lost my phone last
night which created a filter through which to experience
the whole day. It was lost when I went to bed, and I felt
the sick feeling of money troubles. When I woke up it
was clear, a beautiful day, and Jack was in my bed. I felt
the simultaneous relief and fear of being separated from
a valuable thing. There was the strong possibility I was
going to have to spend a lot of money to replace my phone,
but yet, I wasn't dead. It was sunny and Jack's body was
just within reach. I laid over him and worried about the
phone and felt his skin – he felt like he'd been drying in
the sun after a swim. It was really bright in the bedroom
but as if a filter had been placed in front of the windows.
Like a photograph. It was soft and a little damp. He
moved, said something toward me, touched me. He held
me against his back and I expressed my worry though he
was still asleep. He was speaking to me in little ways, with
his head and his hand, through a dream. Everything felt
possible. But that's looking back. Now I sit here with my
stupid phone and I could call anyone I want. It's Mother's
Day. It's been so all day.

We got up and used the bathroom, washed our hands,
brushed, lay back on the bed. I called the movie theater
on Jack's phone and left a message. We started having sex.
But, we decided, we'd better walk over there and check,
then we can come home and shower and have sex and do

some work before Jack would have to get on the road. We took the dog, I wore a skirt, a really flowy one with dark flowers on it that came just above my knees and felt like a kitchen rag that had been worn thin and a black tank top and brown vest and two gold bracelets that fell down against my palm while I walked. Jack held the leash. I braided my hair which I'm doing more. Jack had on jeans and said it feels like 70. It was 70, we had checked before we left. I'd said it felt a little cold when we started walking, but we were wearing different things. Jack seemed to be saying that degrees are objective. Later in the day he told me a story about the placebo effect. We were sitting outside just off Fulton, at the little tables in the triangle between the intersection, and he said that across the board the color of the pill makes a difference, has the same effect. Blue sleeping pills work better, everywhere in the world except for Italy. In Italy (just for the men) blue sleeping pills work less.

It's getting dark now I can't believe this day is over. This day was maybe four or five days and they were all Mother's Day, I kept reminding myself, because usually it's just one day.

Most of the day felt like a different era. A time before this time. When we walked to the theater I just knew the way. Jack had forgotten though we'd been there the night before, but he doesn't live here all the time. It had felt like he did for a few days so I was surprised when he kept going straight. We had to turn left. The doors were open, this was a good sign. I felt a bit of relief and anticipation. Jack and the dog waited outside. I was inside a long time and he was outside sitting on the stone banister of the steps, it fit his body perfectly and the dog was happy to stand by his side as he looked at his phone or the people passing on their Sunday way. When I got back out I had a whole story for him about Felix, the security guard who let me peek inside even though he wasn't supposed to and how I'd had to lay on the floor of the theater to see fully under the seats – though I didn't actually tell Jack this bit because I knew he would find it gross – that the phone was nowhere to be found but Felix had taken my number (Jack's number) and a description of the phone to give the manager when he got in around 1 or 1:30. We wondered what to do until then, it was only 10:30, and soon we said let's go find some breakfast up that way. We talked and the sun was in our faces. Someone said my name. It was a friend from school, coming through the intersection towards us. She was headed to the Botanic Gardens and then Hong Kong in a few days for good. I told her about the phone and we were going to breakfast and she said we should come by the Gardens later but I knew we wouldn't be able. I told her we had to wait for the manager but really we had to go back and spend the last hours doing things like work and sex and showering. It was too much to explain why but I liked the fantasy of showing up at the Botanic Gardens without a phone and meeting up, the way we used to just meet up or bump into someone, the way the days felt like many things could happen, unplanned and unexpected, like they were many days in one.

We went to the bagel place for breakfast and it took a long time. Jack came in while I was waiting for our order to ask what was wrong – but nothing was wrong, I was just waiting and I had sunscreen in my eye. He handed me a napkin from his pocket and went back to the dog. I wiped my eye while the girl rang me up saying the kitchen was slow and they must have gone to Australia for our cheese. I didn't get her comment, about Australia and cheese, it kept me wondering for a few minutes, and a bit later in the day I thought of it again. Australia was a long way away, but was there a cheese connection that I wasn't getting? It was the second time in two days I'd heard someone use Australia as an example of a far away place. The other person to make that reference was the friend we'd run into in the intersection, though that was two nights ago. They were right, it is far, but it still seemed strange. We ate our sandwiches at the tables where we talked about placebos a few minutes later. Jack forgot something he was about to say and we waited silently looking at each other for him to remember.

We decided it would be a while, the manager calling, and Jack needed to get some work done but it didn't make sense to go all the way home. He asked if I had a book with me and somehow I didn't, though I almost always do, but it hadn't seemed important, when we left my apartment we left in such a breeze, I felt a little sleepy and worried, my skin a soft fabric, same as my skirt and Jack kept touching me on the shoulders, it was all so easy I just left wearing thin shoes and no sweater without double checking my purse. I could just leave things, I could stumble outside, which I never do, and things would go on, the day would go on and we'd do things or they'd happen. This was the whole day, Mother's Day 2014, but it was really a much longer time in some other dimension, some other fashion. A quick dream of my life. You wake up and the dream has happened in six minutes or something because you looked at the clock just before and then drifted off again and this whole thing happened.

One of my favorite bookstores was just down the street. It was so fortunate, everything happening one after the other. Jack would stay with the dog and I'd walk over and pick up a small, cheap paperback, there were always things I wanted, something little I could read in a few hours sitting outside at the tables while Jack did work. We would just sit there until the manager called, hopefully with news of the phone. There was the little anxious feeling underneath everything, that they wouldn't have it, but the phone was starting to feel distant and as I walked across to the bookstore I had the most free feeling. Jack would be waiting for me at the tables, but if he wasn't I could probably find him, at the theater or my apartment, even if it took us hours to find each other, we had time, even though he had to leave in a few hours, it felt like the day might go on forever and somewhere in the city I would find him easily. I felt like I could walk forever, even though I had my purse over my shoulder, my skirt felt like air, the same as the air on my shoulders that Jack had been touching at the tables and in my apartment and the bookstore was just down the block with its big glass windows, even though I probably shouldn't be spending money in case I had to buy a new phone, it felt like it didn't matter and I was confident I would find something cheap and perfect. I knew some people who worked at this bookstore but I didn't think they would be there on a Sunday. When I walked in, one of them was at the counter. He looked right at me, right away and said hey and I said hi, I'm just looking for a book do you have any recommendations and he said always, but I let him finish with his customer. He found me at the chapbook table that he'd set up earlier, it was easy to feel connected to each other with the whole rest of the store seeming unimportant and this table seeming like the place to be, like the whole store was on this table and we both knew it. We talked about a few of the books, the good ones that were obvious and then some others, and we talked about each other to each other, about what we were doing and about the summer coming up and what we'd be doing then, as far as we could tell. We talked about writing and then he went to help a customer and I looked at more books. I picked the one he'd recommended and another by Perec I'd been meaning to read and kept running into but never bought, once because it was eight dollars and the clerk wouldn't take the seven I had on me, though it was used and he had the authority. The books were not inexpensive but it didn't matter. I had a credit card and the day would go on forever. I still hadn't called my mother but I didn't have a phone. I needed to call her before Jack left so I could use his phone. I was worried about the call and doing it before Jack left and about the fact that it was Mother's Day and yet all these other things were happening. I was worried I'd been away from Jack too long. When I left the book store he came into view across the street. He didn't see me. I watched him at the table, staring out from the table at the view. I could tell from how he was sitting that he was wondering what was taking so long, maybe not at that very minute, but in general. I could tell he had been wondering that and maybe getting a little anxious for me to come back. I looked at him until he looked over, the light was red. He waved very friendly and then went back to his phone, relaxed, knowing I would cross soon.

Neither of us got very far – me in my book or Jack in his work – before the manager called. Something had distracted us, it was the dog. Jack fed her some ice from his cup and she started choking. She was heaving and heaving but nothing came up, she wasn't breathing. I started to feel panic, but I didn't show it. It's important to stay calm around dogs, especially if there's something wrong. Jack stood over her with his hand on her side and waited. Eventually, foamy yellow vomit came out. She shook her head to get it off because dogs can't spit, so it went everywhere, it was almost comic except I was worried she was choking for real and I was trying to remember what to do when a dog is choking, running through the list of things I'd looked up in the past, trying to be prepared for a crisis. Soon she was just sniffing the flowers by the table, as if nothing had happened. I asked Jack for a napkin and he produced one from his back pocket. I wiped the foam off her lips and walked to the trash to throw it out. She tried to follow me and the chair tipped over. Jack set it right. We just looked at each other for a while, said that was nasty, what happened, I guess she choked on the ice. As soon as we started reading again, the manager called. But it wasn't the manager, it was Felix, the security guard. He asked me to describe my phone and when I did he said, I think I have it. I was so happy, but I could feel myself putting it on, even though I really was relieved. Maybe I wasn't happy, I couldn't tell if I was happy or not, suddenly my book seemed pointless, even though I still wanted to read it. Thank you Felix, thank you so much. I was overdoing it, like the phone was a member of my family. He said come to the stage door and I asked where. 116 St. Felix street. When I told Jack the address, for a minute I thought I'd gotten his name wrong, called him Felix by accident which would be a strange name to call someone if it wasn't really their name. Jack said, his name is St. Felix? He was joking but he also wanted an answer. I guess it's just a coincidence, I said, should we go over? Yeah, Jack said, let's go get it. I undid the leash and my purse from the chair and left the table.

We went to the wrong door, it was locked. Felix came walking down the street. He said, see those little stairs right down there? Go knock on that door, he has your phone in an envelope. I thanked him again, put my hand against my chest, over the heart, which felt like a version of hugging, like the equivalent of hugging him though to hug him would have been inappropriate and overboard. I wasn't sure I was even happy, but I was grateful and relieved. I was also happy. They asked for my ID, which is a fake ID – not a fake but a fake address, or an address that doesn't belong to me anymore. He had me sign the envelope, which seemed pointless, and we left. I almost dropped the phone coming down the little stairs out front and Jack laughed. The case was on backwards, this was a mystery, and the battery was dead, but we already knew that from trying to call it. Though when I got home and plugged it in it came right on, the battery wasn't dead, it had been turned off or something. It worked fine. It was just like it had always been.

After Jack left I wanted to stay outside. My apartment is always so dead right after he goes, walking back from the gas station and seeing his car drive off, getting faster as it goes down the avenue toward the freeway toward some-where else. I stayed with him until the last moment, the gas station, the short ride over, walking to the car, as he packed. It was soon after we had sex that he felt anxious to leave. It was getting later, he'd wanted to leave earlier in the day but the phone dilemma had kept him. I did not take this personally, though I felt it like a formation inside me. He had a long drive back and lots of work to get done. I wanted him to be safe getting home, not to get tired halfway through and call me saying he was falling asleep, as he sometimes did. He had almost fallen asleep after we had sex, but he forced himself up and out of bed. Just before that he was lying behind me, touching my arms and hips which were exposed and the top of my stomach and just under my breasts where my shirt had come up. My skirt was around the middle of my waist and still felt like nothing against me, even the elastic part. He kissed me on my neck and back where my hair was off to the side. He'd really liked it when I bit his ear this time, I'd bit it hard, he didn't used to like that, or at least he didn't care one way or the other, but this time he liked it, the timing of it did something different and he'd moved me off him quickly and gotten on top from behind. I still hadn't called my mother, but I had my phone back so I could call anytime. I thought maybe we'd call together after we got dressed, on video so she could see us – she'd like that better – but everything was so rushed after that I forgot until I was walking to the diner and Jack had left. I had such a craving for a cheeseburger.

I passed the diner once because the tables by the open doors still had food left on them. I'd give them a minute to clean up, or I wouldn't go back, I'd just keep walking the dog forever, but I couldn't do that because I felt faint and then almost panicky with hunger, fatigue, the numbness in my skin still there. I had put the skirt and tank top back on though they smelled like sex. What's that smell like, Jack asked me when I told him how they smelled. You know, I said, but I didn't really either, it was just something someone had said to me once, that I smelled like sex. It was in a CVS. My cousin turned to me while we were squatting down in front of the pregnancy tests. She was thinking of buying one and we were wondering which was the best, so we went in for a closer look and that's when she said I smelled like sex, though I didn't believe it, not literally, because I'd been telling her that Jack had just left and I think this gave her the idea to say it, after all I'd showered before I met up with her, but I got what she meant, in the figurative sense, the way someone says it reeks of whatever in here – you stink of fear, or the smell of success. But of course there is a sex smell, a way that sex smells, and I felt a little self-conscious sitting at the tables so close together. On one side of me was a table with two women who looked like sisters and seemed so happy about everything they were saying, as though they were faking it for each other, or exaggerating in order to convince themselves that the day was a great day and everything was going so well, and beneath this was a genuine pleasure in being together, but it was a struggle to express this, they felt the need to express it instead of simply sitting in their pleasure together.

On the other side was a threesome, two men and a woman. She was French. I could tell from her accent, plus she looked French, something in the mouth, the way she held the corners of her mouth, as though her teeth wanted to burst through at any moment as she spoke in her endearing accent and it seemed like the man on the other side of the table, the one who wasn't her boyfriend but her boy-friend's friend, was falling in love with her a little bit. Then the boyfriend did something odd, he said he had to go pick up his shoes and he pointed to the cobbler across the street. I'm never here, he said, when that guy's open. He keeps weird hours and is always closing right before I get there and since I'm coming from work I can never get there early. Plus he's not open on Saturdays either. It's his business, he can do what he wants, but anyway, I need to go get them, do you mind. The woman and other man shook their heads, sure, that's fine. Hopefully I'll come back with nicer shoes, he said, but several minutes later he was still gone, and then their food came and the woman said I'm so hungry and the friend said, you should eat, go ahead. She looked across the street towards the direction her boyfriend had gone. Please, eat, you're hungry, the friend said. I'll eat too, he won't mind if we eat before he gets back. They really seemed to enjoy their food. My food hadn't come. I was reading the Perec which reminded me to notice everything that was going on. There was a little girl throwing a tantrum on her mom's lap and the mom just laughed and laughed at her husband who laughed back but was looking at his phone. Eventually the girl went to the bar and spun around on the red stools. I purposefully noticed her for a while and then looked around the diner for something else to notice. I followed the waiters, looked outside, tried to watch everything. But, I'm a woman, I thought, though I wasn't sure why. The French woman and the friend were still alone, trying to make conversation, though she was doing the heavy lifting. He was absolutely awkward and as he became more and more smitten he was unable to propel the conversation forward even a little bit. She asked him about his job. My cheeseburger arrived but it was a hamburger. The waiter left too fast and I was hungry so I ate it without cheese. She was giving him advice about how to respond to someone, a colleague, saying he should be direct and get what he wants or something like that. Everything she said sounded like a romantic gesture, though it was not, but he allowed it to become one, nodding and smiling at her. He would do exactly what she said – even if he did not. Her boyfriend was still getting his shoes and she tried to make conversation about the park. Perec was listing buses by their numbers, and describing the pastries the passersby had. I switched to my French fries for a while. The dog tried to come into the restaurant to eat food that had fallen on the floor. I pushed her back. The boyfriend returned and sighed heavily but he had nothing. No shoes, no bag. He didn't explain himself. His girlfriend and friend kept talking as if he hadn't sat down. The friend would have sex with her right now if she would let him, but she probably would not. I went back to the hamburger. This half was bigger and would have been far better with cheese. I realized, again, I'd neglected to call my mother. I wondered how she was doing, but I didn't want to make that call in public. The boyfriend and his friend were talking about the weight they'd lost, they started listing their numbers: 250 to 215, 315 in high school, then 275, now 210. The worst thing is when you start feeling good about yourself, the boyfriend said. Then you think, I can have something, I can have whatever I want, just once. But the trouble is doing that every day, if you have what you want every day then you're in trouble. The friend agreed. The French woman asked him to take their picture. I looked at the boyfriend's stomach and wondered if they got married would he gain all the weight back? Would she be disappointed?

It took some time to get the check. I knew they were closing but they didn't seem concerned about me sitting there reading, sipping my coffee slowly. Finally, the waiter caught my eye from across the diner and made the gesture, the check gesture, and I nodded and smiled. I was supposed to do that, though I never felt right doing it, feeling that it was rude to ask someone with your hand in the air to wait on you. I paid, I asked for change. He brought me a five and a one which made it difficult to tip. I thought maybe I had another bill in my wallet. The table of sisters had gone. The waiter was saying something to me. Do you like chocolate? I nodded and he reached into a box by the register, handed me a chocolate lollipop shaped like a flower, a tulip on a stick, but flat, wrapped in a little cellophane and a yellow ribbon. I thanked him and put it in my purse. I considered giving him the five, but then I'd have paid him for the chocolate, which he gave me maybe to flirt, or because it was Mother's Day and they just had them or because he felt sorry for me sitting alone, as if he was saying here, you shouldn't be eating alone, but I wanted to be eating alone, and what, I wondered, would he have thought if I'd been older, or fatter, would he have given me a chocolate then? Perec wasn't handed chocolates by his waiters. It was nice, but it was different. It was impossible to blend in alone. Perec sat for three days in the café eating sausage sandwiches, drinking beer and coffee, writing, and just staring for large swaths of time between entries, for 45 minutes sometimes he'd sit and stare at things from the café and no one said anything, and no one gave him things or wondered about him or noticed him, he was invisible and he could even enter the ladies room undetected and see what the ladies were doing, peep on the ladies while they removed their underthings to sit on the cold, white seats of the public restroom and relieve themselves while they talked through the stalls about the people at their table, which he didn't know they did – talking through the stalls over the sounds of their own peeing and then continuing the conversation as they came out and washed their hands and fixed their hair or picked a bit of seasoning from their teeth or spat in the sink and gurgled water and spat again or added make-up to their already made-up faces. He could see everything and nothing saw him, except through his own observations, imagining himself through his own eyes, a self-determined self, a solid self, documenting changes as they swirled around him, as his coffee or beer changed the scene before him, a stationary eye, status absolute, the swarming birds, the same birds each day, the same square, different happenings.

Thank you to Tony Iantosca, Daniel Owen, Jack Russo, Sarah Anne Wallen, and Lewis Warsh, for your feedback, support, and inspiration.

Special thank you to Leo Madriz for making the cover art with such care and intention – and for helping me figure out what this book is about.

Parts of Morning Ritual have previously appeared in *The Portable Boog Reader 8* and *Poems by Sunday*.

Lisa Rogal was born in Pittsburgh, Pennsylvania. Her writing has appeared in *Lungfull!*, *Greetings*, *Poems by Sunday*, *Brooklyn Paramount*, *Boog City*, and *By the Overpass*. In addition to *Morning Ritual*, she has published translations of poet Vladimir Druk in *The Days are Getting Longer* (Third Floor Apartment Press, 2013), and a chapbook, *The New Realities* (Third Floor Apartment Press, 2014). She is a graduate of the MFA program at Long Island University and currently lives in Brooklyn.